CELEBRATE

CELEBRATE

DISCOVERING JOY IN LIFE'S ORDINARY MOMENTS

Margaret Feinberg

Foreword by Luci Swindoll

THOMAS NELSON
Since 1798

NASHVILLE   DALLAS   MEXICO CITY   RIO DE JANEIRO

Published in Nashville, Tennessee, by Thomas Nelson. Thomas Nelson is a trademark of Thomas Nelson, Inc.

Thomas Nelson, Inc., titles may be purchased in bulk for educational, business, fund-raising, or sales promotional use. For information, please e-mail SpecialMarkets@ThomasNelson.com.

Unless otherwise noted, all Scripture quotations are taken from THE NEW KING JAMES VERSION. ©1982 by Thomas Nelson, Inc. Used by permission. All rights reserved.

Scripture quotations marked NIV are taken from HOLY BIBLE: NEW INTERNATIONAL VERSION®. ©1973, 1978, 1984 by International Bible Society. Used by permission of Zondervan Publishing House. All rights reserved.

ISBN: 978-1-4185-4928-2

Printed in China

11 12 13 14 RRD 5 4 3 2 1

Contents

Contents

Foreword

A number of years ago I had two cats. More accurately, they had me. I've never purposely had a pet in my life, but these two little fractious felines made my front porch their home. They showed up one morning when I was leaving for a walk, demanding food and attention, neither of which I was prepared to give. Nor did I want to. I didn't like cats. At least, I hadn't up to that point, and through the years had been mercilessly criticized by my cat-loving friends who considered me to be an otherwise compassionate person. I held to the belief that cats were too independent to belong to an already independent individual. Nevertheless, here they were at breakfast time, staring at me imploringly. I remembered that amusing book by Jack Smith, *Cats, Dogs and Other Strangers At My Door* where he talks about various animals who had without invitation intruded into his life, warmed themselves by his fire and won their way into his heart. Lost in these musings, I went on my walk, leaving the strangers at my door, unattended. They weren't happy, but so what? I owed them nothing.

It wasn't until I got home that I gave them another thought, and that was because the fatter of the two cats was poised on top of the second floor air-conditioner, looking down on me in deep contemplation. She really was rather cute, so I decided to capture her in celluloid. I dashed in the house, grabbed my camera, and just as I leaned into a somewhat awkward position to get the right angle for the picture, I threw my back out. I could hardly move because of the pain. No matter how I turned, I was miserable. I glanced up to the air-conditioner just in time to see the cat leave and come down to where I was writhing. It was at that moment, strangely enough, I decided to name her Ms Ree because she wanted to be with me. Ms Ree loved company! The affection between us had begun. Her inscrutable name fit her perfectly and no matter what I was doing she was by my side.

The other cat, younger and friskier of the two, followed Ms Ree everywhere. I named her Shadow, because indeed she was that to Ms Ree and ultimately, to me. I loved those cats to pieces. I fed them, bought them toys, fixed a little place for them to sleep on the porch, and in gratitude, they left me a dead mouse one day on the Welcome mat.

What is it about ordinary things in life that give us so much joy? Just this morning I stood at the window overlooking my back yard and watched a beautiful cardinal flitting around from tree to tree. I was mesmerized for ten or fifteen minutes. It was as though my entire yard belonged to him. God has invited us to enjoy these gifts of beauty and uniqueness. They remind us that He is present in the ordinary moments of life. All we have to do is take time to focus and enjoy them.

In this Study Guide, you're going to read about various backgrounds and conditions in which you'll see God in unique ways. So often we think we have to buy something to give us joy, or plan a party so we can celebrate. And some of us can't be happy if we're alone. But, I can tell you from experience, many of the richest and most enjoyable moments I have, happen when I'm by myself; when I concentrate on what is right in front of me; when I stop and look up, or around; when I forget about me and think about the other person. And here's the fun of it: It's free. It's daily. It's everywhere. You don't need money, fame, education, or a proper setting to discover the joy in life that's there for the taking. All you need is to open your eyes and heart.

Even when you're *"served up a plate full of misery"* as Job, the patriarch of the Old Testament says, there are moments of relief and beauty if you look for them. The Lord Himself is your Shadow. And it is He who reveals them to you.

—LUCI SWINDOLL

Introduction

God's Invitation to You

Do all the good you can, by all the means you can, in all the ways you can, in all the places you can, at all the times you can, to all the people you can, as long as ever you can.

JOHN WESLEY,
THEOLOGIAN

God is issuing you an invitation to a celebration that is just too good to miss! Right here, right now, even in the midst of the challenges you face every day, God is waiting for you to say yes to begin celebrating the joy in your life.

Sometimes we can miss out on the celebration simply because we spend too much time and energy waiting to be happy. You may be tempted to tell yourself that the real celebration will begin . . . *when I meet Mr. Right . . . when I land the promotion . . . when the kids are grown . . . when I retire . . .* Yet, as the weeks roll into months, and the months roll into years, we can miss out on celebrating the blessings God has placed right in front of us. We can spend so much of our lives waiting to be happy, that we miss out on laying hold of the joy that God has for us each and every day.

All we need is a change in perspective—knowing where (and how) to look for God's blessings in your life and celebrating with a thankful heart. Before you know it, you'll start celebrating the joys that have been hiding in plain sight. You'll discover there's more to celebrate than you ever imagined.

Celebration is contagious. As you begin celebrating the work God is doing in your life, it won't be long until others notice and join in the party. You'll find that once you start celebrating, it's hard not to bubble over with generosity and hope. Like confetti, gratitude and appreciation will fill the air. You'll be grateful you said yes to God's invitation.

My hope and prayer is that, throughout this study, you rediscover the joy that comes with being a child of God and that, in response, you'll find yourself inviting others to celebrate the goodness of God, too.

Blessings,
Margaret Feinberg

Saying Yes to All God Has for You

Did you know that God wants to do abundantly more for you than you ever expected or imagined? God wants to throw you a party in which He gives you divine gifts—the presents (and presence) of contentment, gratitude, joy, and thanksgiving in your life.

One

Unwrapping the Gift of Contentment

*There are two ways to get enough: one
is to continue to accumulate more and
more. The other is to desire less.*

G. K. CHESTERTON,
ENGLISH WRITER

A story is told of a wise man who traveled around giving away his gift of wise words for free to anyone who asked him. Upon entering a remote village, the wise man was greeted by a local man who was standing in his yard waving his hands wildly.

The local man explained the challenges he faced in his small one-bedroom home. Though he worked hard, his family shared a very small space. Recently, he'd had several arguments with his wife and didn't know how to improve his marriage or create a sense of peace in the home.

The wise man noticed several chickens and a goat in the yard. "Do you have any animals other than these?" he asked.

The villager said that he also had a sheep, two dogs, and a cat. "Place them inside the house with you!" the wise man advised.

The wise man noticed some tools in the yard. "Do you have any tools other than these?" he asked.

Desperate to help his family, the villager did exactly as advised.

The villager said that he had a few more he stored behind his house. "Place them inside the house with you!" the wise man advised.

The wise man noticed a pile of leaves and dead branches in the corner of the yard. "Do you have any other leaves or branches than these?" he asked.

The villager looked at him hesitantly and said that he had another pile in the back. "Place them inside the house with you!" the wise man advised.

"I'll be back in three days to check on you," said the wise man before disappearing down the road.

Desperate to help his family, the villager did exactly as advised. Three days later, the wise man reappeared as promised.

The villager ran toward him and complained that everything had become worse. The animals were making a mess of the house. The tools were taking up too much space. The leaves and branches left dirt everywhere. Their house was a disaster, and everyone was unhappy.

"Remove everything you brought in, and I'll return tomorrow," the wise man said, before turning and walking away.

Though frustrated, the villager did as he was instructed. The next day, when the wise man reappeared, the villager had a sparkle in his eye and a huge grin on his face as he proudly announced that the house felt so much bigger, cleaner, and quieter now that everything was removed. He and his wife were delighted to have their home back. The wise man smiled and walked away.

This story illustrates that sometimes the only difference between contentment and discontentment is a shift in perspective. Nothing changed for the villager except for his outlook. Unwrapping the gift of contentment that God wants to give us often requires a change in perspective. We need to look to God to be reminded of what's truly important, recognize what lasts forever, and identify what has real value in our world. God desires that we don't experience contentment as a passing fancy or fad, but instead that we live out of a deep sense of contentment that permeates our lives, our attitudes, and our relationships.

1. *Imagine that you were the villager and the wise man had advised you to bring your possessions inside from your yard, your car, or your workplace for three days and then remove them. What do you think the experience would teach you? What would be the most difficult aspect of those three days? What would be the easiest aspect of those three days?*

2. On the continuum below, how content are you in your life right now? Explain.

1——2——3——4——5——6——7——8——9——10

| |

I am extremely
discontent in my life.

I am extremely
content in my life.

3. In what areas of your life do you tend to struggle with contentment the most? Place a check by any of the following that apply. Explain your selections.

____ Financial/Wealth

____ Relationships/Friendships

____ Health/Wellness

____ Status/Titles

____ Age or Stage in Life

____ Others

The book of Proverbs, usually attributed to Solomon, is known for its words of wisdom. Proverbs offers various sayings and aphorisms still repeated and cherished today. Proverbs 15 uses the metaphor of a feast to show the difference between contentment and discontentment.

4. Read **Proverbs 15:15–17**. *In what ways have you found these proverbs to be true in your life over the course of the last three months? When are you most likely to forget the truth of these proverbs in your everyday life?*

The Psalms comprise a collection of songs of thanksgiving, hymns, laments, and other types of ancient Hebrew poetry. While a large portion of the book of Psalms is attributed to David, many of its authors are unknown. Psalm 131 is a song of trust—its author encourages believers to be content in all circumstances.

5. Read **Psalm 131**. *Which phrases from this brief Psalm speak directly to the issue of contentment? How did the Psalmist cultivate the gift of contentment in his life, according to this passage? Which practices suggested in this passage can help you cultivate the gift of contentment in your own life?*

The apostle Paul talked about discovering contentment in every circumstance—not just when things were going well but also when he faced challenges and difficulty.

6. Read **Philippians 4:10–13**. *According to this passage, what is the secret to finding contentment in every circumstance? Why is it important to discover contentment that is not based on circumstances?*

Paul's letter to Timothy encouraged him to stick to the things that bring contentment in life: godly living and sound doctrine. He also urged Timothy to avoid the earthly desires that lead to discontentment.

7. Read **1 Timothy 6:3–21**. *In the first column below, make a list of things mentioned in this passage that increase contentment in everyday life. In the second column below, make a list of things mentioned in this passage that decrease contentment in everyday life.*

Increase Contentment	Decrease Contentment
Ex: Remembering we brought nothing into this world and can carry nothing out	Ex: Desiring to be rich

8. *What steps can you take over the upcoming week to intentionally embrace the gift of contentment in your life?*

> *When we unwrap the gift of contentment in our lives, our focus shifts from trying to achieve or acquire more to celebrating all that we've been given.*

Digging Deeper

The author of Hebrews echoes Paul's warning to Timothy against the love of money and encourages the readers to be content with what they have. Read **Hebrews 13:5–8**. Reflecting on this passage, how has God shown Himself faithful to you? In what specific ways have you discovered God as your helper? Who has demonstrated and inspired you to live a life of godly contentment? Prayerfully consider any areas of your life where God is calling you into greater contentment.

Bonus Activity

Purchase a journal or use a few pages in a journal you already own to make a list of things for which you are grateful. Add at least ten specific things to the list each day. Reflect on God's presence in your life and celebrate God's faithfulness. Thank God for all He has done and all He has yet to do in your life. Celebrate the reasons for contentment in your life.

Two

Discovering the Gift of Gratitude

We can only be said to be alive in those moments
when our hearts are conscious of our treasures.

THORNTON WILDER,
AMERICAN PLAYWRIGHT AND NOVELIST

A simple word of thanks can go a long way toward making some-one's day. Whether the word of gratitude is expressed in a hand-written note or a hallway conversation in which someone pulls you aside to share their appreciation, these words of affirmation are powerful. They are powerful not just when you receive them, but also when you give them.

Some scientists believe that gratitude is essential to happiness.[1] In fact, a group of scientists have engaged in a long-term research project exploring the effects of gratitude on health and well-being. The researchers found that people who are grateful have higher life satisfaction and positive opinions as well as lower levels of depres-sion and stress.

Among case study participants who kept a gratitude journal on a weekly basis, most felt better about their lives as a whole and were more optimistic about the upcoming week when compared to those who only wrote down their difficulties or daily events. Scientists are proving what many of us have known all along: Gratitude can increase enthusiasm, determination, attentiveness, and energy. In other words, gratitude is good for the soul.

Gratitude can increase enthusiasm, determination, attentiveness, and energy.

Despite the benefits of gratitude, cultural anthropologists have noted that some cultures don't even have a word for thanks. While saying thank you may be ingrained in our culture as an expression of politeness and civility, some cultures don't use the word *thanks* at all.

Maybe that's because gratitude goes beyond the words *thank you* and reaches into the heart. Popular author Thomas Merton once noted, "To be grateful is to recognize the love of God in everything He has given us—and He has given us everything. Every breath we draw is a gift of His love, every moment of existence is a grace, for it brings with it immense graces from Him."[2]

Merton pointed out that gratitude takes nothing for granted but is always awakened to the wonder and awe of God's goodness. Those who are grateful discover God's goodness not just through mental assertion or belief but by experiencing the goodness of God in their lives. God desires for us to discover the gift of gratitude in our lives—a gift that, like contentment, truly keeps on giving.

1. Name five things that you're grateful for in your life right now. Say each one aloud.

2. How does saying aloud what you're grateful for affect your emotions, your perspective, or how you feel about life?

3. In the last 72 hours, when have you told someone thank you or been told thank you in a significant way? Describe the experience. How did you feel afterward?

4. When, in the last week, did you miss the opportunity to be grateful? What was the effect on yourself? Your relationships?

5. According to each of the following passages, when can thanks be offered to God?

Psalm 119:62:

1 Chronicles 23:30:

Philemon 1:4:

1 Thessalonians 1:2:

2 Timothy 1:3:

When are you most likely to offer thanks to God in your own life?

6. Look up each of the following passages. What do each of the following encourage us to give thanks for?

1 Chronicles 16:34–35:

Psalm 30:4:

Psalm 119:7:

Psalm 136:1–3:

Isaiah 12:1:

2 Corinthians 2:14:

1 Timothy 2:1:

For what are you most likely to offer thanks to God in your own life?

7. *What happens to your relationships with God and with others when you express approval, appreciation, and gratitude?*

8. *What practical steps can you take over the upcoming week to be more intentional about being grateful to God and others?*

> *When we discover the gift of gratitude in our lives, we realize that it's a gift that keeps on giving. The more grateful we are, the more grateful we become.*

Digging Deeper

Paul offered instructions to the church in Thessalonica specifically regarding their attitudes toward God. Read 1 Thessalonians 5:18. Reflecting on this passage, in what kinds of moments or situations in your own life do you find it easiest to express thanks to God? When is it the most difficult for you to express thanks to God? Prayerfully consider how you can express gratitude to God even in the midst of these challenges.

Bonus Activity

Last week's bonus activity encouraged you to purchase a journal and record specific things for which you're grateful daily. Continue the practice this week by adding more each day. At the end of the week, reflect on everything you've written down. Prayerfully reflect on how your level of contentment and gratitude has changed since you began the journal.

Three

Rediscovering the Gift of Love

*For the love of God is broader, Than the
measures of man's mind; And the heart of
the Eternal is most wonderfully kind.*

F.W. FABER,
BRITISH THEOLOGIAN

Built more than fifteen hundred years ago, the mausoleum of Galla
Placidia still stands in Ravenna, Italy, as one of the best preserved of
all the mosaic monuments.[1] Walking into the small building, built by
the emperor of Rome for his sister, is an unusual experience. Though
historians herald the wonders of this structure, most tourists are surprised by how little one can see when walking inside.

The building has only a few small windows. The scant rays of
sunlight that illuminate this ancient building are often blocked by
crowds of tourists who come to see this ancient wonder. Travelers
who are in in a rush will often miss the beauty inside. Crammed into
the tight, stuffy space, many take a quick glance before scurrying
back outside. However, those who linger often discover a hidden secret. Alongside the wall is an easy to overlook metal box. Whenever

a visitor drops a coin inside, the lights suddenly flip on for a few brief moments, illuminating the lustrous tiles of the mosaic. The dark blue dome comes to life with twinkling stars that cause even the most tired traveler to ooh and ahh at the breathtaking scenes. A deer drinks from a spring. Fruit and leaves hang ripe—ready to be plucked. Jesus reaches out tenderly to one of his sheep. As quickly as the lights turned on, they turn back off, and visitors are left in a room that seems darker than when they walked in. Yet those who have caught a glimpse of the wonder of the mausoleum walk away with an unabashed sense of delight in the discovery.

The truth that God loves us is not only foundational but also eternal.

Like wandering into a dark mausoleum and discovering a beautiful, illuminated mosaic, we can find ourselves in awe whenever the lights turn on in our spiritual lives and we catch another glimpse of just how much God loves us. In those moments, it's hard to not to be overwhelmed with contentment, gratitude, delight, and joy. The truth that God loves us is not only foundational but also eternal. Of all the gifts that God gives us, the greatest is his love. We were created both out of love and for love. Apart from the love of God, it's impossible for us to walk fully into everything God has for us. So even if you've discovered God's love for you, it's a gift worth rediscovering each and every day of your life.

1. *Like the tourists visiting the Galla Placidia, when did you first experience God's love being illuminated or becoming real to you in your life? Describe the moment.*

2. *In your everyday life, what types of situations or interactions make the love of God the most real to you?*

3. *What situation in the last three months has tempted you to doubt, question, or even forget God's love the most?*

The book of Romans is known for being Paul's systematic theology. While written to the church in Rome so long ago, the words and ideas in this letter still resonate with churches and believers today. Romans 8 expresses the depth and transcendence of the love of God.

4. Read **Romans 8:35–39.** What 17 things does this passage say cannot separate us from the love of God? Fill in the chart below.

What Can't Separate Us from God's Love?	
1	Ex: Tribulation
2	
3	
4	
5	
6	
7	
8	
9	
10	
11	
12	
13	
14	
15	
16	
17	

5. *Reflecting on the list you've created from Romans 8, which of these things tempts you to second-guess or lose track of God's love the most? Explain.*

The idea of justification through Christ's death on the cross is a consistent theme throughout Romans. Paul reminds readers of the beautiful picture of love found in Christ's death for us, the unrighteous.

6. *Read* **Romans 5:6–8.** *According to this passage, what is one of the most significant signs of God's love for you? What does it mean to you to lay down your life for someone else? Other than Christ Himself, who in your life has made a significant sacrifice on your behalf? Describe.*

John makes it very clear in 1 John 4 the source of—and reason for—love. To love is to offer evidence of our association with God. We love because God first loved us. John says that by loving others, we are able to know and see God.

7. Read *1 John 4:7–12*. In what ways is our love for one another a reflection of our love for God? Describe a moment in the past month when you chose to love someone because you loved God.

8. What are some practical ways you can keep the reality of God's love alive in your heart? What are some practical ways you can build up others in the reality of God's love?

> *When we discover the gift of God's love in our lives, we realize that it's a gift we simply can't keep to ourselves. We must pass it on.*

Digging Deeper

John reminds us that true love overcomes all fear. While it may seem natural to be afraid and fearful concerning love, God's love is not something we should be afraid of. Read 1 John 4:18–21. Reflecting on this passage, when have you experienced the presence of love triumphing over fear? How would you define the love of God? What does this passage reveal about the love of God? Why do you think the love of God is so important? What would life apart from the love of God look like?

Bonus Activity

Make a list of five people to whom you would like to express the love of God over the course of the next week. After you record their names, write down the words or actions that you would use to demonstrate that love and be intentional about sharing God's love with each person. When you gather next week, share your experiences with the group.

Four

Sharing the Gift of Generosity

*Let no one ever come to you without leaving
better and happier. Be the living expression
of God's kindness: kindness in your face,
kindness in your eyes, kindness in your smile.*

MOTHER TERESA,
NOBEL PEACE PRIZE WINNER

When we discover the gifts of contentment, gratitude, and love in our lives, we can't help but overflow with generosity in response to all we've received. Generosity literally springs up inside of us because we can't contain it. How much generosity is bubbling up inside of you? Take The Full o' Generosity Quiz and find out!

The Full o' Generosity Quiz

1. *Your best friend's birthday is tomorrow! You are anxious because:*

   a. *You need more time. You have no idea what she wants and you haven't had time to find out. You'll grab a gift card for her favorite coffee store in the morning.*

   b. *You've secretly been asking around about what she really wants. Now all you've got to do is wrap it, write a personal note in the card, and wait to see the smile on her face.*

   c. *You've had her present purchased, wrapped, and the birthday card filled out for weeks. You can't wait to see the sparkle in her eye when she unwraps what you already know is the world's best gift.*

2. *The doorbell rings and you discover a young neighbor boy on your doorstep. You've known his parents for years. When you invite him in, he pulls a catalog out of his backpack. He needs to sell just a few more items as part of a fundraiser in order to meet his sports team's requirement. You respond by:*

   a. *Telling the young boy that you're not interested now but would love for him to come by the next time he has a fundraiser.*

   b. *Asking him about his sales goals and how close he is to meeting them, then purchase a few items you know you can use for stocking stuffers at Christmas time.*

   c. *Offering the young boy a snack and drink as you review the catalog and purchase quite a few items so that he'll beat his sales goals and be able to get home earlier tonight.*

3. *It's volunteer cleaning day this Saturday at your church. You've got a busy weekend, but you know that every extra set of hands can make a difference. You decide to:*

   a. *Bake some brownies and cupcakes to drop off for the volunteers because you know snacks are always welcome.*

   b. *Carve out a few hours in the morning to stop by to wash windows, dust floorboards, and clean out some closets.*

   c. *Round up a few friends and spend half the day laughing and enjoying each other's company as you wash, scrub, and do everything you can to leave the church clean and shiny.*

Scoring

Tally up the total number of A's, B's, and C's.

If your answers are mostly A's, you're a naturally generous person. You like to give, but sometimes circumstances and time constraints make it difficult for you to give as much as you'd like. Still that doesn't deter you from practicing generosity.

If your answers are mostly B's, you can't help but bubble over with generosity. You naturally think about how you can help serve, make other people feel comfortable, and share your love in a tangible way.

God wants to fill you with His generosity.

If your answers are mostly C's, you're abounding with generosity, sometimes even at your own expense. If you see a need, you jump at the chance to fill it and even bring in others to help out. You're always going above and beyond to demonstrate kindness and love, but sometimes you need to take a step back and allow others to show kindness and love to you.

No matter what you scored today or this week, know that God wants to fill you with His generosity—a kind of generous response that exudes God's love and radiates joy.

1. Did anything surprise you or catch your attention about your personal results for The Full o' Generosity Quiz? If so, explain.

2. What are some common barriers you've faced in your life when it comes to being generous? What types of situations tend to make practicing generosity more difficult?

3. Do you think it's possible to be generous to a fault? Why or why not? Have you ever had an experience in which you or someone you know was overly generous and it had an unhealthy effect on your life? If so, describe.

God is outrageously generous. Anything we can offer to someone else, God first gave to us. God invites us to reflect his generosity with others.

4. *Look up the following passages, and record what each one reveals about the generosity of God.*

   Psalm 145:16:

   Matthew 6:31–33:

   Matthew 7:11:

5. *Reflecting on these passages, in what ways have you experienced the generosity of God in a meaningful way in your life?*

6. *Look up each of the following passages. What promises does God make to the generous?*

   Proverbs 11:25:

   Malachi 3:10:

   2 Corinthians 9:10–11:

   Proverbs 19:17:

7. *Which of these passages have you found to be true in your life in a meaningful way? Explain.*

Many people think of money or finances when they think of generosity, but God wants us to expand our understanding and expressions of generosity.

8. *Which of the following have you felt challenged to become more generous with over the course of the last year? What was the result?*

Free time

Volunteer time

Family time

Wisdom and knowledge

Passions and personal talents

When we discover the gift of God's generosity in our lives, we can't help giving to others. Generosity is contagious.

Digging Deeper

Joseph of Arimathea was presumably from the enemy's camp. Though he was part of the council that condemned Jesus to death on the cross, Joseph boldly asked Pilate to bury Jesus' body properly. Read Mark 15:42–46. Reflecting on this passage, what was so generous about Joseph of Arimathea's actions? When have you felt a clear prompting to do something generous for someone else? How did you respond? Have you ever felt compelled to do something generous for someone else but failed to act? How did the decision affect you? How did the decision affect the other person? Ask God to give you opportunities to express his generosity over the course of the next week.

Bonus Activity

Make a list of three people who you know who have pressing needs in their lives. Their needs may be for financial support, work, childcare, friendship, or simply time to get away. Prayerfully consider how you can be an answer to those needs by offering an act of kindness, a gift, an encouraging word, or a listening ear. Share your experiences with the group the following week.

Throwing Confetti Alongside a God Who Celebrates

How often do we sit down and reflect on how much God has been and is doing in our lives? Sometimes it's mindboggling to think about all of God's involvement and faithfulness. God isn't in just the big events but in the smallest details as well. When we take time to remember and reflect on what God has done, we can't help but celebrate.

Five

Celebrating Through Remembrance

Christc has turned all our sunsets into dawns.

CLEMENT OF ALEXANDRIA,
CHRISTIAN THEOLOGIAN

Have you ever been on a long road trip? Hopping in the car with friends or family and driving hundreds of miles can be a whole lot of fun. New sights and adventures wait with each passing mile. But sometimes on a road trip, we become so concerned with the destination that we miss out on the joys and delights that accompany the journey.

In the same way, sometimes we speed through life without taking time to reflect on all we've seen, experienced, and learned along the way. That's one reason it's important to take time not only to reflect on our lives and where we've been but also to remember God's presence throughout the journey.

While many lessons in this study begin by telling someone else's story, this lesson is about you and your story. You're invited to remember all the ways God has been with you, revealing his faithfulness and goodness over the years. To help you remember God's involvement in your life, fill out the chart below. Use each letter of the alphabet from A to Z to write down a word or phrase that describes a moment in your life or an experience that revealed God's faithfulness to you. You may want to write a person's name, a place you lived or worked, or an experience in which God revealed himself more deeply to you.

A	
B	
C	
D	
E	
F	
G	
H	
I	
J	
K	
L	
M	
N	
O	
P	
Q	
R	
S	
T	
U	

V	
W	
X	
Y	
Z	

When we take a few moments to remember God in specific moments of our lives, it's amazing to see God's goodness and faithfulness in ways we may have forgotten. These remembrances become reasons to celebrate God even more.

1. *What did the list you made of God's faithfulness in specific moments of your life reveal about your own faith journey?*

2. *Were there any surprising or long-forgotten moments that came to mind as you developed the list? If so, explain.*

3. What are three benefits of remembering and celebrating God's faithfulness in your life?

Early in the history of the Israelites, they were living in Egypt as slaves under the authority of Pharaoh. They were forced to work long hours under abusive conditions until God selected Moses as a leader to deliver them out of Egypt and the bondage of slavery into a promised land all their own. The Israelites spent forty years in the desert before they came to the border of the land God had long promised them. Before they crossed into the land, Moses delivered some specific instructions and called them to remember all God had done over the years.

*4. Read **Deuteronomy 8:1–9**. Make a list of the things Moses reminded the Israelites of in the space below. What did each item reveal about the character, faithfulness, and intent of God?*

Despite God's faithfulness, God knew that the Israelites were prone to forget his commandments and presence in their lives.

5. Read **Deuteronomy 8:10–18**. According to this passage, what temptations would cause the Israelites to stop remembering and obeying God? Do you think people still face these temptations today? Why or why not?

6. In your own life, what kinds of situations or circumstances tempt you to forget God?

7. Read **Deuteronomy 8:19–20**. What are the consequences of forgetting God? Have you or someone you know ever forgotten God and found your lives negatively affected? If so, explain. Why do you think God is so adamant about remembering and obeying him alone?

One of the greatest things about being a child of God is that we don't have to make the journey of faith alone. We get to live out our faith among fellow believers. And we have the opportunity to celebrate God's faithfulness and goodness together.

8. *What are some ways you can be more intentional about remembering and celebrating God's faithfulness in your life? What are some ways you can be more intentional about helping others remember and celebrate God's faithfulness in their lives?*

One of the most powerful ways we can celebrate God's presence in our lives is simply by remembering his involvement in specific moments. When we remember God's faithfulness in the past, we can trust God even more confidently with our futures.

Digging Deeper

Jesus introduced the Holy Spirit and explained the Spirit's role in our lives in John 14. Read **John 14:26**. Reflecting on this passage, what role does the Holy Spirit play in helping you remember God's faithfulness, presence, and voice in your life? When are you most likely to ask God's Spirit to help you remember God in your life? When are you least likely to ask God's Spirit to help you remember God? Spend some time asking the Holy Spirit to do exactly what Jesus promised in this passage—to teach you and bring to mind things God has revealed to you in the past that are important to your journey now.

Bonus Activity

During the introduction of this lesson, you began making a list of specific moments in which God had revealed himself to you. Over the course of the upcoming week, continue growing the list by adding three to five more moments each day. Use the journal that you have used throughout this study. Prayerfully ask the Holy Spirit to bring to mind instances of God's faithfulness, and share one particularly meaningful moment with the group the next time you're gathered together.

Six

Celebrating Through Experiences

*Faith is to believe what we do not see, and the
reward of this faith is to see what we believe.*

AUGUSTINE,
THEOLOGIAN

The deepest part of the world's oceans is found in the Pacific Ocean off the coast of Guam.[1] It's known as the Mariana Trench, and it's the lowest elevation of the Earth's crust, estimated to be nearly 36,000 feet deep. That's nearly 7 miles down. To put this in perspective, Mount Everest is the highest mountain in the world at 29,029 feet. If you placed Mount Everest in the deepest crevices of the Mariana Trench, you'd still have more than a mile of water above it.

While multiple attempts have been made to explore the Mariana Trench, only three have been successful. The first was on January 23, 1960, when Jacques Piccard and Donald Walsh courageously climbed into a Swiss-designed, Italian-built submersible boat. The duo descended into the cold darkness at a rate of three feet per second. The descent took nearly five hours. They touched down in the Challenger Deep—the deepest part of the Mariana Trench.

They spent nearly twenty minutes on the ocean floor—a place where the surrounding water has a pressure of 15,931 pounds per square inch. Despite the immense pressure, Piccard and Walsh were delighted to find a fish that looked like sole or flounder pass by as well as a shrimp. In the midst of the cold darkness, they discovered life.

The same God who spoke, led, protected, and guided those in the Bible, speaks, leads, protects, and guides us.

Though two other descents—one in 1996 and another in 2009—successfully made it to the Challenger Deep of the Mariana Trench, these expeditions were unmanned. Piccard and Walsh remain the only two to have made the journey and experienced the beauty and depths of the Mariana Trench firsthand.

Sometimes, if we're not careful, we can find ourselves reading the Bible in the same way we read the story of Piccard and Walsh. Though their story is real and well-documented, it feels distant and impossible to most of us. We can't fathom going to the bottom of the Mariana Trench. Such a feat is something that *they* could do but *we* could never do.

God never intended us to read the Scripture or live out our faith that way. Instead, God wants us to read the Bible with the expectation and faith that the same God who revealed Himself to men and women throughout the Scriptures wants to reveal Himself to us. The same God who spoke, led, protected, and guided those in the Bible, speaks, leads, protects, and guides us.

One of the ways God goes out of His way to communicate this truth is by having people go beyond listening to actually experiencing the Word, truth, and stories of God. God wants us to taste and see that the Lord is good! Throughout the Old Testament, God called people to festivals and celebrations like Passover and

Pentecost, and in the New Testament, Jesus asked His disciples to break bread and drink from the cup in remembrance of Him through Holy Communion. Each of these experiences is a reminder that our God is the same yesterday, today, and forever. The great things God did in the past, God can do again today in our lives—and that's worth celebrating!

1. *When you read or listen to the stories of what God did in Scripture, do those stories simply seem like distant things God did for people long ago? Or do you tend to think those stories apply to ways God is working in your life today? Explain.*

2. *Which amazing stories in the Old Testament are easiest for you to relate to and see the connection with how God is working in your life today? Which in the New Testament?*

3. Which amazing stories in the Old Testament are the hardest for you to relate to and see the connection with how God is working in your life today? In the New Testament?

In the book of Exodus, we discover one of the central celebrations of the Jewish faith: Passover. Pharaoh enslaved the Israelites, and Moses was selected by God to demand the Israelites' release. When Pharaoh refused, ten plagues fell upon Egypt. The waters of Egypt turned to blood. Frogs, gnats, and flies invaded the land. Diseases and natural disasters abounded. Only after the firstborn of every Egyptian family died did Pharaoh agree to set the Israelites free.

The Jewish holiday of Passover is a time of remembrance and celebration for the evening the angel of death visited Egypt but "passed over" the homes of Israelites, whose doorposts were marked with the blood of sacrificed lambs. The Passover celebration doesn't just commemorate the lamb sacrifice but also the speed at which God's people were released. They literally left their homes so quickly that they didn't have time for their bread to rise. Thus, to this day, Jews eat unleavened bread, also known as *matzah*, during Passover.

4. Read **Exodus 12:1–29.** Why do you think God instructed the Israelites to commemorate this defining event? (Hint: Exodus 12:14)

5. What did the Passover reveal about the character of God including God's power, faithfulness, and strength?

6. What lessons or insights from the Passover story apply to your own spiritual journey right now?

Just as God instructed the Israelites to celebrate the Passover as a way to re-live and remember the faithfulness of God, Jesus also instructed His followers to remember Him through the celebration of the Eucharist or Holy Communion. The Gospels note that Jesus' instruction to partake of the bread and wine happened during Passover and allude to the fact that Jesus was becoming the sacrificial lamb that would take away the sins of the world to save people.

7. *Read **Mark 14:12–26**. Why do you think Jesus gave His disciples the instruction to eat and drink these foods in remembrance of Him? When you take communion what do you remember or reflect on concerning Jesus?*

8. *On the following chart, place a check mark by the spiritual disciplines that have helped you or continue to help you to grow in your faith and truly taste and see that the Lord is good. Then place a plus mark by the spiritual disciplines which you haven't found as effective for you in the past but you'd like to grow in for the future. What steps can you take to be more intentional about*

growing in your relationship with God and celebrating the realities of God in your life?

__ Holy Communion	__ Service
__ Silence	__ Fasting
__ Baptism	__ Fellowship
__ Giving	__ Confession
__ Prayer	__ Scripture Memory
__ Worship	__ Liturgy
__ Scripture Reading	__ Other

God desires for us to celebrate His faithfulness and goodness by tasting and seeing that the Lord is good through spiritual disciplines and sacraments like Holy Communion.

Digging Deeper

Numbers 15 points out a strategy for the Israelites as well as a symbol of consecration to the Lord. Read **Numbers 15:37–41.** Reflecting on this passage, why do you think God instructed the Israelites to place tassels on the corner of their garments (also known as *tzitziyot*)? What is the purpose of the tassels according to this passage? What kinds of modern-day tassels do you have in your life to help you remember God?

Bonus Activity

Reflect on the spiritual disciplines from the final question in this lesson. Which were the most unfamiliar or difficult for you to incorporate in your own spiritual life? Over the course of the next week, research one or two of these spiritual disciplines in depth by going online or to a local library with a good selection of Christian books. Prayerfully consider trying a spiritual discipline that may have been challenging or difficult for you in the past. Share your experiences with the group the next time you gather.

Seven

Celebrating Through Rest

*The Sabbath is our way of acknowledging that
life is a gift and this world and its blessings
are not the result of the work of our hands.*

STEPHEN SHOEMAKER,
PROFESSOR AND AUTHOR

Throwing a great party involves planning, hard work, and attention
to detail, but the results are often well worth the investment! Party
planners suggest the best recipe for a great party begins with rounding
up the help of a few friends. Two or three people pitching in can really
lighten the load for everyone. Together, you can brainstorm themes
and discuss decorations. Everyone can offer input on the best location
and time for the gathering. And, of course, you can talk about food!
Will everyone bring something to the party? Will you each divide up
cooking duties? Should you plan on an affordable catering option?

Once the details are decided, party planners say it's time to spread
the word with invitations by phone, online, and in person. Make sure
to think through the timing of serving food and dessert as well as how
to handle parking, if you have lots of guests. Then prepare to have fun!

Celebrate

One of the hallmarks of a great celebration is that it often looks effortless, though a whole lot of hard work is involved. Creating a guest list, purchasing decorations, and preparing food are no small matters—even when you have the help of friends.

Did you know there's a party God is throwing that doesn't involve a lot of work for you? It's actually a celebration of rest. You're invited to be a special guest.

Since the beginning of time, God has been throwing the celebration of rest for all of humanity. In fact, to celebrate the wonders of creation in Genesis 1, God actually took a day off to enjoy the wonder and beauty of all that had been made. Imagine for a moment: God has just finished placing fluorescent fish at the bottom of the sea and hanging stars in the sky. Everything is awhirl in awe of what God has done. As a holy exclamation point for the seventh day, God doesn't work harder or tweak His design. Instead, God takes a day off to celebrate creation with rest.

God doesn't just take the seventh day off to demonstrate what rest looks like; God takes the seventh day off to invite us to celebrate life with rest on a regular basis. God invites us to enter His rest so that we are refreshed, rejuvenated, and bubbling with new life. Though your calendar may be full, the celebration of rest is a party you can't afford to miss.

1. *When was the last time you threw a party for someone? What was the occasion? What made the party memorable? Did the event make you tired or recharge you? Explain.*

2. *On the continuum below, how easy or difficult is it for you to take time to rest in your life right now? Explain.*

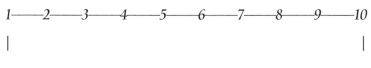

It is extremely difficult
to take time to rest.

It is extremely easy
to take time to rest.

3. *What are some of the biggest barriers for you when it comes to making time to rest in your life right now?*

After six amazing days of creation, God chose to rest on the seventh day. It's worth noting that in the description of the seventh day, the actual words seventh day are mentioned three times. No other day of creation is mentioned as many times as the seventh day. While we don't know why the seventh day is mentioned three times, the repetition suggests its importance. The groundwork was being laid for honoring the Sabbath. God set apart the seventh day as holy. This was the first of many things which God would set apart to Himself, but as the first thing He set apart, the Sabbath deserves special attention.

4. Read **Genesis 2:1–2**. What was God's attitude toward the seventh day? What do His actions on the seventh day reveal about the character of God? What do God's actions on the seventh day reveal about the importance of rest?

Rest isn't just an invitation but a command. When Moses received the Ten Commandments, the fourth was that we should remember the Sabbath by keeping it holy. Scholars suggest that the first four of the commandments deal with our relationship with God while the last six focus more on our relationships with other people—though the commandments invariably affect both our relationship with God and others.

5. Take turns reading **Exodus 20:1–20**. Why do you think rest is so important to God? When are you most likely to be too busy to rest? What happens in your own life when you refuse to rest?

6. *How does rest recalibrate your relationship with God, others, and work?*

The invitation to rest is clearly identified in Matthew 11. Jesus understands the heavy yoke of the world—how tired and burdened people become. He offers His yoke instead. A yoke is the wood that joins two animals that pull heavy loads. The yoke offered by Jesus is not a heavy yoke of slavery, but one that is light, easy, and offers rest—a stark contrast to the burdening yoke of the world.

7. *Read Matthew 11:28–30. To whom does Jesus issue the invitation to rest? Is it easier for you to say yes to **recreation** or to the **re-creation** through rest that Jesus is offering you in this passage? Explain. Do you really believe that resting can glorify God? Why or why not?*

8. *What steps can you take to be more intentional about entering God's rest in your own daily life? What do you need to be more intentional about doing or not doing in your weekly schedule?*

> *The invitation to celebrate through rest is one that we can't afford to ignore. God invites us to rest and discover Him as our provider, sustainer, and joy of our lives.*

Digging Deeper

Psalm 31 is a psalm of deliverance in which the psalmist seeks refuge in God. Read **Psalm 31:14–15.** Reflecting on this passage, do you tend to trust God with your time or believe that your time is your own? How does taking a day off or remembering a Sabbath affect the way you see time? How does taking a day off affect the way you see God as your sustainer and provider? How does resting increase your appreciation and adoration of God and all that He's given you?

Bonus Activity

Open up your daily planner or calendar and carve out time to rest during the upcoming week. Even if it's only a few hours, make time to unplug and do nothing. You might find it's a little harder than you thought! Take a nap. Sit and reflect. Enjoy the stillness and ask God to infuse you with His rest and presence. Share your experience with the group during the next gathering.

Eight

Celebrating Through Sharing

Joys divided are increased.

JOSIA GILBERT HOLLAND,
AMERICAN NOVELIST

Albert Lexie is known for keeping a regular schedule. Twice a week for more than three decades, Lexie leaves his house at 5:50 in the morning in order to catch a bus to work. But Lexie's is no ordinary job. He travels an hour and a half by bus to Pittsburgh, Pennsylvania, where he works as a shoe shiner in a Children's Hospital. In fact, Lexie uses the same shoeshine box he built in his high school shop class.

Each customer is charged the same fee of $3 to have their shoes shined. What makes Lexie's work remarkable is that he donates all his tips to the Children's Free Care Fund, ensuring that children can receive the medical care they need even if their parents can't pay for it.

Over the last three decades, Lexie has given more than $100,000 to the children's fund. Though his annual income is only $10,000 each year, he gives around the same amount annually to the hospital. Lexie's life is a compelling demonstration of commitment and generosity to those less fortunate.[1]

Lexie's story reveals some of the common misperceptions and myths about giving and sharing, namely, that you have to have a lot in order to give a lot or make a big difference. Though Lexie didn't have what many would consider a significant income, he chose to share what he had and the impact was tremendous. Lexie's story is also inspiring because he didn't wait to share with others. Instead, Lexie shared faithfully for years from his hard-earned tips, and all those ones and fives added up to something priceless: children getting the medical care they needed.

Sharing fills our lives with joy as we reflect God's love and faithfulness to others.

As children of God, we're called and created to share what we have with others. When we act with generosity, we reflect the generosity that God has already shown us. All good things come from God, and when we share what we have with others, we're sharing the goodness of God. At times, we may be tempted to hold back or refuse to give. In those moments, the Bible teaches us that those who share will prosper and those who refresh others will be refreshed themselves (Proverbs 11:25).

So why share what you have with others? Because sharing is one way we fulfill the greatest commandments to love God and to love others. Sharing allows us to put our faith into practice and opens doors of opportunity to be used by God to help meet other people's needs. Sharing fills our lives with joy as we reflect God's love and faithfulness to others. One of the greatest ways we can celebrate our faith is through sharing. Most people discover that once you start sharing, it's hard to stop!

1. *What do you find most surprising or compelling about Albert Lexie's story?*

2. *When have you been on the receiving end of someone else's sharing? How did the situation make you feel toward sharing with others?*

One of the most inspiring acts of contagious sharing is found in 1 Chronicles 29 when gifts were being given for the building of the temple. King David recognized that his own son, Solomon, was the one God chose to build the temple. However, David couldn't help expressing his gratitude to God by contributing to the building fund.

3. *Read 1 Chronicles 29:1–9. How did David's sharing inspire others to give? What was the emotional response of all the people to giving? (Hint: 1 Chronicles 29:9)*

4. How does sharing usually make you feel? Do you think God created us so that sharing with others would be a joyous celebration? Why or why not? Have you ever shared with others and not experienced satisfaction, joy, or delight? If so, explain.

5. After everyone gave generously to the temple building project, David offered his response. Read **1 Chronicles 29:10–20.** How did David respond to the contagious sharing that had taken place among God's people? What was David's attitude toward the ability to share? Toward the acts of generosity? Toward God?

6. Who do you know whose life is marked by sharing what they have with others? Without saying the person's name, what are some of the hallmarks of a life marked by sharing?

7. Using your imagination, what would a person's life look like if they lacked any sense of generosity or willingness to share? How would this impact their life? Relationships? Faith?

8. What are some common barriers to practicing contagious sharing? How can you be intentional about overcoming any barriers to sharing in your life right now?

The invitation to celebrate the goodness of God through sharing with others is extended each and every day. We can share our gifts, talents, time, and resources to serve and love others.

Digging Deeper

Paul encouraged the Christians in Corinth to graciously and cheerfully share out of what they had. He reminded them that they should share as freely as possible. Read **2 Corinthians 9:6.** Reflecting on this passage, in what way have you found this principle to be true in your own life? When you're making everyday decisions, when are you most likely to think about this principle? When have you reaped generously in your own life? When have you sown generously? Spend some time asking God to make this principle more vibrant in your own spiritual journey.

Bonus Activity

Over the course of the next week, do something outrageously generous and completely unexpected for someone else. You may choose to spend an afternoon babysitting or offer to wash a neighbor's car. Send a handwritten letter to someone you know expressing gratitude for their involvement in your life. Share in a specific way to meet someone's needs and take note of the joy and thankfulness you feel in your own heart.

Bubbling Over with Celebration Everyday

Celebrating the goodness of God isn't just reserved for specific holidays. God's presence isn't just available one particular day of the week. The joy we find in God isn't just meant for a few hours of the day. As children of God, we're invited to celebrate the wonders of God every day. We're meant to bubble over with the strength, hope, goodness, and life God wants to give us and, in the process, share them with others.

Nine

Bubbling Over With Strength

*The way to grow strong in Christ is
to become weak in yourself.*

C.H. SPURGEON,
PASTOR

Hugh McColl isn't your average 90-year-old. While others may celebrate their birthdays with a gathering of friends and family, McColl simply decided to step into the ring . . . the boxing ring, that is! It's a sport and activity McColl has enjoyed for years.

What makes McColl's enthusiasm for the sport unusual is that he didn't strap on a pair of boxing gloves for the first time until he was 75. Growing up, McColl had enjoyed watching boxing and always knew the sport required hard physical work and training. During retirement, he decided to try to boxing as a way to stay in shape. Fifteen years later, he is still boxing at least once a week. In an interview with the *Edmonton Sun*, McColl said he hopes to continue training and still be stepping into the ring on his 100th birthday.[1]

McColl's enthusiasm and tenacity are an inspiration. At 90 years old, he reminds us that though we often think of strength as being physical, strength is far more than what can be measured in muscles. Strength is demonstrated in our attitudes, actions, and approach to life.

At times, we may feel weak and tired, tempted to step out of the ring and call it quits. The daunting tasks and obstacles before us may discourage us, but even in those moments, God desires to be the source of our strength.

The Apostle Paul wrote, "I can do all things through Christ who strengthens me" (Philippians 4:13). Paul discovered that no matter what he was facing, God wanted to strengthen and empower him as an overcomer. No matter what the hurdle or challenges, God wanted to be the source of everything Paul needed to persevere and endure. And God wants to be our source of strength as well.

In fact, when we're at our weakest, God desires to be our greatest strength. That may seem counterintuitive, but throughout the Scriptures, God repeatedly demonstrates that when we *can't,* God *can.* Throughout the Psalms, God reveals himself as a rock, a fortress, a shield, and a stronghold (Psalm 18:2), all of which are symbols of strength and power. All of these images also reveal God as a source of protection. So if you find yourself feeling weak, know that God not only wants to strengthen you but protect you and glorify Himself through you.

1. What inspires you most about McColl's story? What do you hope your life will look like if you live to be 90 or even 100 years old?

2. *When you wake up most days, do you tend to feel strong or weak?*
Mark your response on the continuum below. Briefly explain your
response.

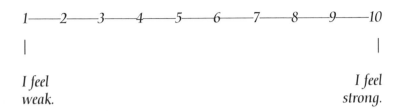

1———2———3———4———5———6———7———8———9———10

I feel
weak.

I feel
strong.

3. *What kinds of situations in life tend to make you feel the most weak*
or vulnerable? When in the last six months have you encountered
a situation that made you feel weak or vulnerable? How did you
respond? How did God reveal Himself in the situation?

4. *Psalm 37 is a Hebrew acrostic poem—meaning each stanza begins*
with the subsequent letter of the Hebrew alphabet. Read **Psalms**
37:39–40. *According to the passage, why does God help and deliver*
His people? What kinds of situations are the most difficult for you to
trust God? What kinds of situations are the easiest for you trust God?

Psalm 18 was written after the Lord delivered David from the hands of Saul. In this Psalm, David expressed the deep intimacy and safety he found in the Lord.

*5. Read **Psalm 18:1–2**. In the chart below, make a list of all the terms mentioned that describe God. Next to each one, record how you've discovered God in each of those ways.*

Description of God	Personal Experience
Ex: Strength	Ex: Shortly after a new job, I was tempted to quit.

6. Read **Psalm 31:24** and **Psalm 105:4**. *Why do you think God wants us to wait on Him and seek His presence continually as a source of strength? Have you ever been tempted to become impatient and trust in your own strength? What was the result?*

Paul faced a challenge in his life that he called a "thorn in the flesh" which left him feeling weak and vulnerable. God's response, however, wasn't to remove the difficulty.

7. Read **2 Corinthians 12:7–10**. *What surprises you most about God's response to Paul's weakness? Describe a time in the last month when you discovered God's grace is sufficient for your weaknesses.*

8. *Where in your own life right now do you most need an infusion of the strength of God? Spend some time asking God to give you strength and to glorify Himself through you.*

> *The invitation to celebrate the strength of God is extended to us every day. God's power is demonstrated in our weakness so we shouldn't be shy about calling on God for strength.*

Digging Deeper

Read Isaiah 40:30–31. Reflecting on this passage, when have you experienced this principle to be true in your own life? Why do you think God draws near the weary and weak? What does this reveal about the character of God? Spend some time asking God to give you strength and for you to be a source of strength to others as well.

Bonus Activity

Over the course of the next week, use a concordance or visit a website like www.biblegateway.com to look up the word "strong" in the Bible. Read through the various passages that reflect on the strength of the Lord and write down those which are most meaningful to you. Share what you learn with the group the next time you gather.

Ten

Bubbling Over with Kindness

*A kind heart is a fountain of gladness, making
everything in its vicinity freshen into smiles.*

WASHINGTON IRVING,
AMERICAN AUTHOR

While attending a three-day women's getaway, Evelyn was challenged by the Biblical teaching she heard and encouraged by the prayer she received. Yet, the moment that meant the most to her was one evening when she returned to her room. She discovered a lovely shawl, tenderly tied with a ribbon, resting on her bed. A note attached to the shawl said that the handmade gift was called a prayer shawl and was meant to be worn whenever she felt sad, worried, anxious, in need of comfort, or anytime she wanted to be reminded of God's enveloping love for her.

Evelyn learned that each woman at the retreat received a prayer shawl of a different color and pattern, and each shawl seemed perfectly matched for its recipient. All of the shawls were hand knitted by a team of women from a local church, who lovingly prayed for each woman as they worked on her unique shawl.

Touched to receive the shawl from people she didn't even know, Evelyn was inspired to begin making prayer shawls for other people. One week later, at her Bible study group, she asked for prayer as she shared her desire to start a prayer shawl ministry. Evelyn began thinking of a new friend who had recently moved to the area. Her husband was diagnosed with leukemia and was starting treatment. Evelyn felt compelled to knit a prayer shawl for her.

". . . and He will always be there to wrap His loving arms around us."

Furiously knitting, she finished the shawl a couple of weeks later and invited a group of women from church to come to her home to pray with her friend. Evelyn presented the woman with the prayer shawl and they all prayed together.

"It's not about the shawl really," Evelyn says. "It's about bringing glory to the Lord as we bring needy women to Him with the shawl. The shawl is a reminder that the Lord is in our lives and we can go to Him at any time, for whatever reason, with any emotion, and He will always be there to wrap His loving arms around us."

Several of the women who gathered to pray decided they wanted to be part of the prayer shawl ministry. In their first meeting, ten women gathered and nearly everyone had someone in mind for whom they wanted to knit a shawl. They compiled a list and sent the names of the recipients to the knitters as a reminder to pray for them as they knitted. Today, the group continues to meet monthly, and the women knit on their own in between group meetings as well.

"It's a ministry to reach those in need and to show care and compassion, but most important[ly], it's a start to bring them to the Lord, who is sovereign over their circumstances and who cares for them personally," Evelyn says. "This is my goal for the prayer shawl ministry. I believe this will be a powerful ministry that the Lord will use to bring people to Himself."

The story of Evelyn and the prayer shawls is knitted with kindness. Someone cared enough to knit a shawl and pray for Evelyn before she ever received it. Evelyn's response was one of passing on the tender loving care. After receiving kindness, she couldn't help but pass it on. Her kindness became contagious. Now, with each prayer shawl the women create, the kindness continues.

Evelyn's story is a reminder that whenever we experience the loving-kindness of God, it's hard not to pass it on. We can celebrate God's kindness by sharing it with others. After all, the kindness God shows to us is too good to keep to ourselves.

1. *Evelyn received a handmade prayer shawl. What is the most meaningful gift that has been given to you?*

2. *What is the kindest thing someone has done for you this year?*

3. How did the act of kindness make you feel? How did the act of kindness affect the way you wanted to treat others?

Kindness can have a bigger impact on our lives than we realize at the time. The women who knitted Evelyn's shawl probably never imagined that their simple but genuine act of kindness would inspire Evelyn to start a prayer shawl ministry of her own and spread kindness to so many others. Yet, all kindness begins with God. He is the one who extends His loving kindness to us.

*4. Read **Ephesians 4:32 and Titus 3:4–6**. According to these passages, who should inspire us to be kind and compassionate to one another?*

5. When, in your own life, do you feel like you have experienced the kindness of God?

In Jeremiah, God clearly states his desire for kindness. The Hebrew word for kindness is *hesed*, meaning loving-kindness, a life characterized by mercy and compassion.

> 6. Read **Jeremiah 9:23–24**. *According to this passage, in what does God delight? Why do you think God delights in kindness? What does this reveal about God's character?*

It can be easy to assume God's judgment is a lack of kindness toward His people. Paul, however, reminds us otherwise in Romans 2. While our actions deserve judgment, God shows mercy, compassion, and loving-kindness in His ability to forgive and in His remarkable sacrifice of His only Son.

> 7. Read **Romans 2:4**. *According to this passage, what is the result of God's kindness? Describe a time when you felt this response to God's kindness in your own life.*

Jesus didn't just demonstrate kindness to us through death and resurrection but also through His life. Jesus challenges us to walk in love and show kindness to those who are unkind to us.

> 8. Read **Luke 6:27–31**. *Without naming a specific person, who in your life is the most challenging to show kindness? Does Jesus' teaching challenge you to respond differently than you have been responding to this person? Explain.*

The invitation to celebrate the kindness of God means that we can reflect God's kindness in our everyday relationships.

Digging Deeper

Sometimes, it becomes easy for us to forget God is the source of all kindness. In their journey to Lystra and Derbe, Paul and Barnabus, who preached the gospel and performed healing miracles for those in need, were considered to be gods by some of those who witnessed their great acts of kindness. They quickly reminded the people that God is the source of all kindness. Read **Acts 14:17**. Reflecting on this passage, what are some of the specific ways you experience the kindness of God in your family, workplace, and daily life? What are some specific ways you can be an example of God's kindness in your family, workplace, and daily life? Spend some time reflecting on the kindness of God in your life and thanking Him for His kindness.

Bonus Activity

Over the course of the next week, memorize 1 Corinthians 13. Start with a few verses a day, and by the end of the week, make an effort to commit the passage to memory. Reflect on the ways you're experiencing and sharing God's love and kindness each day.

Eleven

Bubbling Over with Hope

*All earthly delights are sweeter in expectation
than in enjoyment; all spiritual pleasures,
more in fruition than in expectation.*

OWEN FELTHAM,
ENGLISH WRITER

Dr. Russell Conwell, the founder of Temple University in Philadelphia, was in a prayer meeting where he asked for people who had faithfully given money away to share their stories. One after the other, men and women shared powerful stories of how God had blessed and provided for them through their giving.[1]

Then a 70-year-old woman spoke up. She explained that she wanted to have a story like everyone else had shared, a story that told of abundance and provision, but she was facing tremendous loss and lack. Though she had saved and skimped throughout the years, maintaining a personal commitment to tithe ten percent of her income, she now was about to lose everything. She had just learned she was losing her job, and she had no other means of support. Her words were greeted with silence and then prayer.

The next morning Dr. Conwell was enjoying lunch with the founder of a local department store. The successful businessman mentioned that his store was about to inaugurate a pension system for their employees. Though they had considered it for years, the details of the plan were finally determined. Later that day, they were going to issue the first pension to a woman who had served their store more than two and a half decades. When his friend said the woman's name, Dr. Conwell recognized it immediately. She was the woman from the prayer meeting the night before.

> *The plans of God are not only good; they're designed to give us a future and they're marked by hope.*

Facing difficult situations and insurmountable odds, the woman had begun to lose hope. Yet God remained faithful. Her needs did not go unnoticed, and through an unexpected turn of events, her needs were met in a beautiful way.

In all of our lives, there will be times when, like the woman in this story, we will be tempted to lose hope. We'll be tempted to believe the untruths that somehow God has forgotten us or our needs have gone unnoticed. But just as in the story of this woman, God is still at work, and often God has something up His sleeve that's beyond anything we could ever imagine.

God invites us to put our hope in Him. Jeremiah 29:11 reminds us that God knows the plans that He has for us even when we don't have a clue. The plans of God are not only good; they're designed to give us a future and they're marked by hope.

When we celebrate all that God has done in the past, our hearts are naturally infused with hope for what God wants to do in the future. God's doesn't want you to have *some* hope but instead to bubble over with divine hope and expectation.

1. *When you face a situation like the woman who was about to lose everything, how do you respond?*

2. *On the continuum below, how much hope do you have in your life right now?*

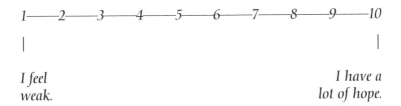

1——2——3——4——5——6——7——8——9——10

| |

I feel   I have a
weak.   lot of hope.

Sometimes we can be tempted to practice hope management, a practice in which we try not to get too hopeful so we don't become too disappointed.

3. *Have you ever practiced hope management? If so, describe. What was the result?*

4. *In the chart below, match the verse to the reference. Of the Scriptures listed, which give you the greatest source of comfort or encouragement in your life right now? Explain.*

Bible Passage	Scripture
Psalm 10:17	The LORD is near to those who have a broken heart, And saves such as have a contrite spirit.
Psalm 34:18	But those who wait on the LORD Shall renew their strength; They shall mount up with wings like eagles, They shall run and not be weary, They shall walk and not faint.
Proverbs 18:10	LORD, You have heard the desire of the humble; You will prepare their heart; You will cause Your ear to hear . . .
Isaiah 40:31	And we know that all things work together for good to those who love God, to those who are the called according to His purpose.
Romans 8:28	The name of the LORD is a strong tower; The righteous run to it and are safe.

While the book of Jeremiah was originally written to God's people in Babylonian captivity, the hope and promise offered in Jeremiah 29:11 still resonates with people today.

5. Read **Jeremiah 29:11**. Describe a time in your life when you questioned whether or not God had a plan for you but discovered God had a plan to give you a future and a hope.

Isaiah 43:1–4 paints a beautiful picture of God's love for his people. God desires a personal relationship with us. He is willing to pay any price for the ones He loves and created.

6. Read **Isaiah 43:1–4**. In the space below, write down any phrases that give you hope for your spiritual journey right now.

7. When you've been in a difficult situation, what is the most hopeful and helpful thing someone has said to you? Why was that statement so meaningful? When you've been in a difficult situation, what is the least hopeful and helpful thing someone has said to you? Why was that statement so unhelpful?

8. *How can you be more intentional about being a source of encouragement and hope for those facing difficult situations?*

> *Hoping in God is a reason to celebrate. God desires to infuse us with hope, not just for today, but for the future He has for us.*

Digging Deeper

Read **2 Corinthians 4:16–18.** Reflecting on this passage, how are you being renewed in your own life right now, day by day? Where, in your own life, do you need to focus more on the eternal than the temporary? In what areas of your life is God asking you to fix your eyes on Him? Spend some time reflecting on the work of renewal and hope God wants to do in different areas of your life.

Bonus Activity

Over the course of the next week, add to the prayer journal you started for the bonus activity in session one. Write down a list of hopes in your life—things you would like to see God do. Then commit these hopes to God in prayer, trusting God to meet you and reveal Himself to you in each of these areas.

Twelve

Bubbling Over with Life

How wonderful it is that nobody need wait a single moment before starting to improve the world.

ANNE FRANK,
AUTHOR

Napoleon Bonaparte is known as a powerful and highly ambitious military leader during the French Revolution. Bonaparte is most remembered for a series of battles he fought known as the Napoleonic Wars in which he conquered much of Europe.

As Bonaparte advanced across the continent, one of his armies discovered a prison that had been used hundreds of years earlier during the Spanish Inquisition. Inside the dungeon, they discovered the remains of a prisoner who had been arrested and imprisoned for his faith. A chain still remained locked around the ankle bone of the skeleton.[1]

Etched into the stone wall beside the remains was the rough image of a cross and four distinct words in Spanish. Above the cross was the word *altura*, or height. Below the cross was the word *profundidad* suggesting depth. To the left of the cross was *anchura* meaning width. And to the right of the cross was *longitud* meaning length.

With these words, the prisoner had left a mark, a witness to the immeasurable love of God. Though the darkness of the dungeon tried to stamp out his hope and faith, the prisoner refused to let go of the abundant life found in Christ. He chose to testify to the greatness of God even in the midst of pain and hardship.

> *We are offered a life free from shame as we learn to grasp the depth of God's love for us.*

No matter what we're facing, God desires for us to celebrate the life in Christ that has been given to us. Jesus promised to give us not just life but abundant life (John 10:10). That means that no matter what curve balls life throws us, Christ is still for us. God wants us to live lives free from shame and walk in wholeness and fullness empowered by the Spirit of God.

Jesus describes the abundant life He offers using shepherding imagery. He describes Himself as the Good Shepherd who has authority to lovingly lead His sheep. It is only through Him that His sheep find lush pasture and safety. Jesus does not offer false hope and assurance like those who come to rob and steal from His sheep. Instead, He offers life to the fullest where His sheep will not lack anything.

Just like the sheep described in John 10, Jesus offers that same abundant life in which we lack nothing, a life in which Jesus provides and protects wholly and completely. We are offered a life free from shame as we learn to grasp the depth of God's love for us.

1. *Reflecting on the story of the prisoner, how has your understanding of God's love deepened or widened since you first met God?*

2. *What types of situations tend to make you question the love of God in your life?*

3. *What situations in your own life in the last six months have made you most aware of God's presence in your life?*

4. *Do you tend to be more aware of God when things in life are going well or difficultly? Explain.*

God's life-giving love is so much greater than we can even imagine! In Paul's letter to the church in Ephesus, he prayed that people would fully grasp the love of God in order to be filled to the fullest extent.

5. *Read **Ephesians 3:7–19**. What is the compelling reason Paul says that he prays? What does Paul ask for? (Hint: Ephesians 3:17)*

6. *In what ways do you feel that Paul's prayer has been answered in your own life? Explain.*

7. Read **John 10:10.** What in your life has turned out better than you ever dreamed? In your own words, what do you think Christ meant when He promised us abundant life?

8. Read **John 3:16–17** and **1 John 3:1.** According to these passages, what does God desire for your life? In what ways do you struggle to realize that God is truly for you?

God desires that we have life and have it to the fullest. God wants us to live lives free from shame and walk in wholeness and fullness empowered by the Holy Spirit.

Digging Deeper

Psalm 37 is an acrostic poem attributed to David (meaning every stanza begins with a subsequent letter of the Hebrew alphabet). David recognized that many evil men seem to prosper; but in this psalm, he encourages the reader to delight themselves in God alone. Read **Psalm 37:3–6.** Reflecting on this passage, how are you delighting in the Lord? What does it mean to commit your ways to Him today? This week? Over the next week, meditate on this passage. Spend time in prayer asking God to teach you what it means to delight yourself in Him alone.

Bonus Activity

Over the course of the next week, revisit the journal you have used throughout this study. Spend time in prayer, writing down your desire to have abundant life in Christ. Think of three people with whom you want to share the message of Christ's abundant life and the everlasting love that He offers. Have a conversation with these friends this week.

Leader's Guide

Chapter 1: Unwrapping the Gift of Contentment

Focus: *When we unwrap the gift of contentment in our lives, our focus shifts from trying to achieve or acquire more to celebrating all that we've been given.*

1. Answers will vary, but usually you would learn to enjoy your space much more without the clutter, even though nothing has changed. The most difficult aspect would likely be the annoyance and frustration with possessions in places they didn't belong. The easiest aspect would likely be the the break you would be forced to take from picking up and organizing.

2. Many participants won't find themselves toward the extremes of this continuum, but this question gets the participants asking themselves about their level of contentment in their lives.

3. While these options are by no means complete, it is easy for us to struggle with contentment in the everyday areas of life.

4. Answers will vary. Being content and cheerful makes all the difference. These proverbs state the difference in outlooks between the people with cheer in their hearts and those who are embittered.

5. The Psalmist talks about keeping a proper perspective rather than being lifted up too high or filled with pride. The Psalmist speaks of being grounded and calmed and quiet in his soul. Like a child who is weaned, he is no longer dependent on someone else for satisfaction or provision. He has found contentment. The Psalmist

reveals the source of his contentment and hope is God, and he calls others, namely Israel, to put their hope in God as well. We can learn from the idea of calming and quieting our souls and not being provoked by looking at what others have or what we don't have. We can stay grounded and not get caught up in things that distract us or draw us away from contentment.

6. *God is the source of our contentment in every circumstance. When we keep our eyes on God, then our contentment isn't based on what we have or don't have, but on God alone. Contentment is something that can be discovered in every situation in life.*

7. *Answers*

Increase Contentment	Decrease Contentment
Ex: Remembering we brought nothing into this world and we can carry nothing out	Ex: Desiring to be rich
Content with food and clothing	Love of money
Righteousness, godliness, faith, love, patience, gentleness	Putting hope in wealth
Place hope in God	

8. *Answers will vary, but choosing to be thankful and grateful for the little things, expressing kindness, and enjoying each moment are helpful. Making it a practice to look beyond our circumstances, focus on God, and remember that His plan transcends our current situations makes all the difference.*

Digging Deeper

This passage is a beautiful reminder of God's unending faithfulness. Answers will vary, but pastors, leaders, teachers, and friends may be some of the people in our lives who have encouraged us to live lives of finding contentment in God.

Chapter 2: Discovering the Gift of Gratitude

Focus: *When we discover the gift of gratitude in our lives, we realize that it's a gift that keeps on giving. The more grateful we are, the more grateful we become.*

1. *Gently encourage participants to share the things for which they are grateful. These may range from nature to their favorite food; others may say their spouse or children.*

2. *Gratitude often lifts our emotions or provides encouragement to our souls as we express gratefulness for what we have been given.*

3. *Encourage participants to share a recent example of gratitude from their own lives. Not all stories will seem remarkable, but remind the participants that this question is designed to get them thinking about gratitude in their own lives. Has it been longer than 72 hours since they have heard thank you either from their own mouths or from another's?*

4. *Encourage the participants to be more aware of being grateful in their lives, so they don't miss any more opportunities.*

5. *Psalm 119:62: At midnight*

   1 Chronicles 23:30: In the morning and evening

   Philemon 1:4: Always

   1 Thessalonians 1:2: Always

   2 Timothy 1:3: Without ceasing; night and day

Answers will vary, but some participants may have set times for prayer or thanksgiving toward God. For others, they may thank God whenever they see fit.

6. *Answers*

1 Chronicles 16:34–35: Thank God for His goodness and enduring mercy

Psalm 30:4: Thank God for His holiness

Psalm 119: 7: Thank God for His righteous judgments

Psalm 136:1–3: Thank God for His goodness and enduring mercy.

Isaiah 12:1: Thank God for His forgiveness and comfort

2 Corinthians 2:14: Thank God for leading us triumphantly

1 Timothy 2:1: Thank God for all people

The participants may have different things to be grateful for (as seen in question one). Encourage them to thank the Lord even for the little things in life.

7. *Answers will vary, but often relationships flourish with others and with God. Everyone enjoys being appreciated!*

8. *Answers will vary, but consider writing thank-you notes in order to be extra intentional about your appreciation throughout the week.*

Digging Deeper

Answers will vary, but it is easy to thank God when things are going well in our lives, and more difficult when we have trials and difficulties

Chapter 3: Rediscovering the Gift of Love

> **Focus:** *When we discover the gift of God's love in our lives, we realize that it's a gift we simply can't keep to ourselves. We must pass it on.*

1. *Some participants may not be able to state an exact time when God's love was illuminated. Others may have an exact moment where they sensed God's love. This question is designed to encourage participants to dive deeper with one another as they journey to understand the love God has for them.*

2. *Some participants may see God's love in nature or in their relationships. Others may see God's love when studying His Word or serving others. God reveals Himself in countless ways. There is not a right or wrong answer.*

3. *Answers will vary. It is easy for us to get overwhelmed by the strains of life to the extent that we forget or doubt God's love. Gently remind the participants that this happens to many people.*

4. *Answers*

What Can't Separate Us from God's Love?			
1	Ex: Tribulation	10	Angels
2	Distress	11	Principalities
3	Persecution	12	Powers
4	Famine	13	Present
5	Nakedness	14	Future
6	Peril	15	Height
7	Sword	16	Depth
8	Death	17	Any other created thing
9	Life		

5. *Answers will vary but moments of loss and difficulties in life can cause us to second-guess God's love.*

6. *Jesus died for us before we knew or loved Him. While we were still in our sins, separated from God, Jesus died that we might be reconciled to God. What an amazing demonstration of love!*

7. *Answers will vary. God is love—therefore by loving others, we reflect the love of God. Sometimes it is hard to love certain people, but we should choose to love them because God loves us first.*

8. *Encourage participants to write down the moments where God's love is illuminated to them so they can return to it whenever they feel doubt or forget.*

Digging Deeper

God's love can be described as boundless, fearless, unconditional, effortless, beautiful, and so on. When we find our worth in God's love, we are better able to love others. Life without God's love would be sad and lonely.

Chapter 4: Sharing the Gift of Generosity

Focus: *When we discover the gift of God's generosity in our lives, we can't help giving to others. Generosity is contagious.*

1. *This fun quiz was designed to get participants engaging with one another. While the results are not scientific by any means, it should give the participant a good idea of where her heart is in regard to generosity.*

2. *Often, generosity is hindered by bad experiences with giving. Sometimes what we have given is abused, causing giving to be difficult. Encourage participants to be honest about what is hindering their generosity.*

3. *This may be a difficult question for some. Encourage participants to share their experiences both bad and good with generosity.*

4. *Answers*

   Psalm 145:16: God satisfies the desire of every living thing.

   Matthew 6:31–33: God knows our needs and meets them all.

   Matthew 7:11: God gives us good gifts.

5. *Answers will vary. God is abundantly generous. Encourage participants to share their experiences when encountering the generosity of God.*

6. *Proverbs 11:25: The generous will prosper; those who refresh will be refreshed.*

   Malachi 3:10: An overflowing of blessing to those who give.

   2 Corinthians 9:10–11: We are given to so we can be generous.

   Proverbs 19:17: Being kind to the poor lends to the Lord, and God rewards this giving.

7. *Answers will vary. Ask participants if there are any other verses left out of question 6 that they would like to add.*

8. *It is important to remember that being generous isn't just financial. Remind the participants that generosity can include their quality time, service, a listening ear, and many other opportunities to be generous.*

Digging Deeper

Jesus' friends and family did not ask for His body; instead a member of the very council that condemned Jesus boldly asked Pilate for a proper burial. In doing so, Joseph put his own life at risk, as he could have been suspected of being a follower of Jesus. In spite of the risks, Joseph decided to honor Jewish law and make sure Jesus' body was buried before the Sabbath. Answers will vary.

Chapter 5: Celebrating Through Remembrance

Focus: *One of the most powerful ways we can celebrate God's presence in our lives is by remembering His involvement in specific moments. When we remember God's faithfulness in the past, we can trust God even more confidently with our futures.*

1. *Celebrate any of the participants' discoveries about God's faithfulness in their lives—from the littlest moments to the greater stories.*

2. *God works in remarkable ways! Sometimes it takes taking a step back to realize the bigger picture of what God has planned.*

3. *Answers will vary, but may include trusting God more, being faithful ourselves, or opportunities to share God's faithfulness to friends.*

4. *Moses reminded the people that God led the Israelites through the wilderness for forty years, thus suggesting God would continue to lead them. The Israelites spent forty years in the desert to be humbled and tested so they would know God. Moses reminded them that God literally provided for them every step of the way. Like a loving father, God disciplined the Israelites. God had a plan for the Israelites to bring them to a land of blessing and abundance.*

5. *Abundance and wealth would lead to pride that would cause the people to forget God. They would deceive themselves into thinking they acquired these things for themselves rather than remembering the faithfulness and provision of God. The temptation to forget God is timeless.*

6. *Answers will vary, but busyness, prayerlessness, lack of gratitude or lack of remembrance can cause us to forget God and His provision and faithfulness in our lives.*

7. *God is adamant about remembering and obeying Him. God forbids following and worshiping other gods because they are false. God demonstrated His faithfulness and presence to the Israelites in the desert for four decades, and He wanted to demonstrate His faithfulness and presence in the Promised Land. However, the Israelites were required to serve and obey Him only.*

8. *Encourage participants to consider journaling. Journaling is a great discipline that allows us to mark all the times of God's faithfulness in our lives. It is a way we can always remember what He has done in our lives.*

Digging Deeper

The Holy Spirit is sent by the Father in the name of Jesus to remind believers of the teachings and life of Jesus. Answers will vary.

Chapter 6: Celebrating Through Experience

Focus: *God desires for us to celebrate His faithfulness and goodness by tasting and seeing that the Lord is good through spiritual disciplines and sacraments like Holy Communion.*

1. *Use this opening question as an ice breaker for the lesson. Sometimes it is easy for us to take ourselves out of the stories in the Bible and assume it was just done for those involved, but be sure to remind participants that these stories, while they happened long ago, are meant as a guide for us to understand how God works in our lives today.*

2. *Answers will vary. Consider stories such as the covenant with Abraham, God leading the Israelites through the desert, David defeating Goliath, the miracles performed by Jesus, and Saul's encounter on the road to Damascus. The list is endless!*

3. *It may be hard to think God can use us in the same ways He used kings and leaders throughout history, but remember God also uses the characters that some may have deemed unworthy or unimportant to take part in His greater story. Consider the stories of David, Ruth, Rahab, Zaccheus, and Stephen. They may not have been the most qualified by the world's standards, but God used them in remarkable ways.*

4. *Answers will vary, but God knew the importance of this moment for the Israelites—it was symbolic of what the Israelites had been through, and also of the great challenges they had yet to face. This was a defining event for the Israelites—a moment that revealed the wonder of God in a powerful way that they couldn't afford to forget.*

5. *The Passover revealed God's power over all of creation. It revealed that God is true to His word. In Exodus 3, God met Moses and committed to set the Israelites free. Now God fulfilled that promise. Nothing can stand in God's way—God is all-powerful, all-knowing, all-loving, and a source of strength in every situation.*

6. *Answers will vary. The Passover story reminds us that God deeply loves and protects His children.*

7. *The instruction to eat and drink is reminiscent of God's instruction regarding the Passover. Like the Passover, the final supper and the sacrifice of Christ is something we can never forget. We need to be reminded of the history of the event as well as the role of God in the event—the power, strength, sacrifice, and love of Christ.*

8. *Encourage participants to choose one of the disciplines listed that is unfamiliar to them, research it, and choose to discipline themselves with that for two weeks. Have them record their insights and experience in a journal.*

Digging Deeper

Tassels were a reminder for the Israelites to remember and obey the commandments of the Lord. God knows we are a forgetful people, so He encourages us to remember Him. Answers will vary, but some participants may place sticky notes of Bible verses around their house or car to remember God's promises. Other people may use landmarks or people to remember to pray. There are many tactics that can be used to jog our memory of God's great promises and love for us.

Chapter 7: Celebrating Through Rest

Focus: *The invitation to celebrate through rest is one that we can't afford to ignore. God invites us to rest and discover Him as the provider, sustainer, and joy of our lives.*

1. *Encourage a vibrant discussion. While parties are fun, they can also be draining on the party planner.*

2. *This question is designed for participants to evaluate how easy it is for them to rest. For some, it may come as second nature, but others may find it extremely difficult with their busy lives and schedules.*

3. *Answers will vary. Life's demands; the power and prestige that come from work; the age and stage in life (such as having a newborn) can make rest difficult.*

4. *God is not anxious, He finds delight and ease in His creation. The world is safely in His hands and will not stop if He rests. The creation of the Sabbath also reveals God's heart toward humanity—one which is not willed toward exploitation but extends the invitation of rest to all.*

5. *It's worth noting that honoring the Sabbath is listed after taking the Lord's name in vain and before honoring your mother and*

father. It's also one of the commandments in which the most detail or background is given. The commandment traces back to creation to suggest that in the beginning God had given the Sabbath to humanity as part of the divine design. Sabbath is very important to God, yet many of us struggle to make time to rest. When we don't rest, we can find ourselves irritable, making poor decisions, more prone to sin, and believing everything depends on us instead of God.

6. *Sabbath can be a healthy way to recalibrate our lives and remember that God is truly the one in control and our source for everything. Rest provides time for reflection, studying God's Word, connecting with others, and an opportunity to recharge. It's also an opportunity to celebrate what God has done in our lives.*

7. *Everyone is invited into God's rest. Yet, often we can find recreation and activities easier to say yes to then carving out the time to enter into the rest God offers.*

8. *Answers will vary. One common reason people don't have time for entering God's rest is over-commitment. Before you agree to another job or volunteer position, carefully consider the time constraints and the need for rest to be a priority in your life.*

Digging Deeper

Answers will vary. It becomes easy for us to think that our time is our own. We jam-pack our days so we are fully taking advantage of all opportunities. However, it is crucial that we take time to rest in God. Rest increases our appreciation and adoration of God. We are more fully able to see the Lord as our sustainer and provider daily when we are renewed in rest.

Chapter 8: Celebrating Through Sharing

Focus: *The invitation to celebrate the goodness of God through sharing with others is extended each and every day. We can share our gifts, talents, time, and resources to serve and love others.*

1. *Use this ice breaker question to open the discussion. Some will be surprised to see how much Lexie shares every year. Others may be impressed by his heart for children.*

2. *Answers will vary. There are many stories—big and small—that are examples of someone sharing. Encourage participants to talk about times when they have seen this in their own lives.*

3. *David's example caused others to give willingly toward the work of the temple including money, gold, silver, and iron. The people gave joyfully.*

4. *Sharing usually makes us feel full of life. God has given us a passion to share and celebrate our generosity. However, some participants may have stories of difficult experiences in which something they shared was taken for granted or even flat-out rejected. Gently encourage them to remember that our sharing is not dependent upon the response of the person or people with whom we have shared. Help them to continue to celebrate their acts of sharing, knowing that they have delighted the Lord with their generosity.*

5. David responded by praising God. David recognized that generosity is only possible because of God who provides all things. He recognized that everything belongs to God and celebrated the joy with which people shared. Then everyone worshiped God.

6. Answers will vary. Encourage participants to think about people in their own lives and families. What stands out about a generous person's personality?

7. Answers will vary. A person who lacks a willingness to share may seem closed off and unfriendly. People wouldn't naturally be drawn to them.

8. Answers will vary. God encourages us to give contagiously and continuously.

Digging Deeper

Answers will vary. Often when we give generously, we are blessed generously. While this may not be the first thought that pops in our head, it is a good reminder that God is faithful to those who are faithful to His Word.

Chapter 9: Bubbling Over with Strength

Focus: *The invitation to celebrate the strength of God is extended to us every day. God's power is demonstrated in our weakness so we shouldn't be shy about calling on God for strength.*

1. *Answers will vary. Encourage a lively discussion.*

2. *This question is designed to have participants assess their strength in everyday life.*

3. *Answers will vary, but challenges include health, finances, and relationships that can leave us feeling vulnerable and weak.*

4. *God saves His people because they trust in Him. Rather than leave God, the people find themselves clinging even more tightly to Him.*

5. *Answers*

Description of God	Personal Experience
Ex: Strength	(Answers will vary)
Rock	
Fortress	
Deliverer	
Refuge	
Shield	
Horn of Salvation	
Stronghold	

Answers will vary. The images of rock, fortress, and stronghold describe God as a place of security from enemies. The Lord as a horn of salvation refers to the horn of an animal that symbolizes victory—God is the source of David's victory.

6. *Waiting and seeking God are a part of the process of being strengthened by God. Ultimately, God desires relationship with us. In the waiting and seeking, we find ourselves strengthened by the very presence of God Himself.*

7. *It's surprising that God didn't just take away the thorn. God left it and used even this to glorify Himself and demonstrate His strength.*

8. *Answers will vary. Spend some time in prayer as a group asking God to show Himself strong in the lives of the participants.*

Digging Deeper

Answers will vary. It is not rare for us to feel weak and weary. God knows our weaknesses and chooses to draw near to us to lift us up. Consider reading the poem "Footprints in the Sand" by Mary Stevenson as a group.

Chapter 10: Bubbling Over with Kindness

Focus: *The invitation to celebrate the kindness of God means that we can reflect God's kindness in our everyday relationships.*

1. *Responses may vary from a physical gift to the gift of simply being present, listening, or journeying through a tough time together.*

2. *Answers will vary, but may include offering to babysit for free, taking the trash out, mowing your lawn, or giving you a listening ear.*

3. *Kindness has a way of catching us off guard and melting our hearts. Kindness tends to be contagious. Once someone shows us kindness, it's sometimes easier to show kindness to others.*

4. *When Jesus came to earth, God displayed His heart of kindness and compassion for the world to see.*

5. *Answers will vary, but God reveals His kindness in many ways daily. The biggest example of this is the gift of salvation in Jesus Christ, but others may include grace, beauty, or creation.*

6. *This passage states that the Lord delights in kindness, justice, and righteousness. Our God is a kind, just, and righteous God, who rejoices in those qualities.*

7. *God's kindness leads to repentance.*

8. *Almost everyone has someone to whom it is difficult to be kind, often because they're unkind. Jesus challenges us to love our enemies and to show kindness even when kindness is not extended to us.*

Digging Deeper

Answers will vary, but may include being more intentional about noticing needs (whether physical, emotional, or relational), and seeing what can be done to meet those needs.

Chapter 11: Bubbling Over with Hope

Focus: *Hoping in God is a reason to celebrate. God desires to infuse us with hope not just for today but for the future He has for us.*

1. *Answers will vary.*

2. *This question is designed to allow participants to evaluate the amount of hope they currently hold onto in their lives.*

3. *Many of us practice hope management unintentionally. While it may decrease our chances of disappointment it also limits our ability to hope and dream.*

4. *Answers*

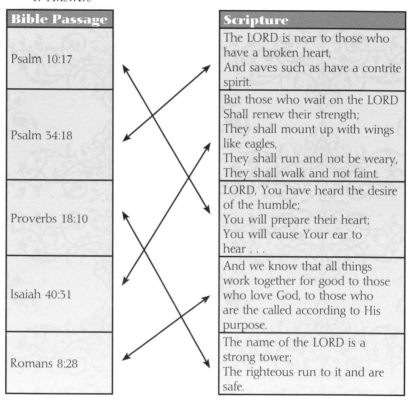

Bible Passage		Scripture
Psalm 10:17		The LORD is near to those who have a broken heart, And saves such as have a contrite spirit.
Psalm 34:18		But those who wait on the LORD Shall renew their strength; They shall mount up with wings like eagles, They shall run and not be weary, They shall walk and not faint.
Proverbs 18:10		LORD, You have heard the desire of the humble; You will prepare their heart; You will cause Your ear to hear . . .
Isaiah 40:31		And we know that all things work together for good to those who love God, to those who are the called according to His purpose.
Romans 8:28		The name of the LORD is a strong tower; The righteous run to it and are safe.

5. *Answers will vary. This is a common question—Does God really have a plan for my life? Remind participants that this promise given to God's people remains true today. God has a plan and purpose for us right now.*

6. *This passage is full of God's love for us. Encourage participants to commit this passage to memory in the upcoming weeks.*

7. *Answers will vary, but it is helpful to remember these things so we can be a blessing and encouragement to others.*

8. *Answers will vary. Noticing those in need of encouragement and hope is the first step. Create a list in your journal or Bible of people who need encouragement and prayer. Consider ways that you are able to encourage and love those people.*

Digging Deeper

Answers will vary. Encourage participants to share their answers with the group. This can become a great conversation-starter.

Chapter 12: Bubbling Over with Life

Focus: *God desires that we have life and have it to the fullest. God wants us to live lives free from shame and walk in wholeness and fullness empowered by the Holy Spirit.*

1. *God's love is revealed to us daily in countless ways. It's amazing to think that we will never fully understand how deep, wide, long, and high the love God has for us is.*

2. *Many times, we tend to associate the love of God with human love, causing us to doubt Him. It is important to remember that God's love is unconditional.*

3. *Examples may include seeing God in friendships, relationships, the workplace, and in nature. God is everywhere all of the time. Encourage participants to seek the Lord in all areas of life.*

4. *It's easy to feel God's presence when things are going well, as opposed to badly. Yet, God is with us in every situation.*

5. *Paul said he prayed so that Christ would dwell in their hearts through faith. He prayed that the people would fully grasp the love of God, so they would be filled with God.*

6. *Encourage participants to give examples of areas in their lives where they have fully understood the depth, width, length, and height of God's love.*

7. *Abundant life may not mean that we have all the material possessions we desire, but that we feel filled by an awareness of the love God has for us.*

8. *God sent His only son so that we may have eternal life. He loves us endlessly and without conditions. Nothing can take away his love for us. God calls us His children.*

Digging Deeper

Answers will vary. Delighting in the Lord may mean to stick to His promises and His law. Putting the Lord's desires first then pulls our desires in line with His.

Notes

Chapter 2

1. http://psychology.ucdavis.edu/Labs/emmons/PWT/index.cfm?Section=4.

2. Merton, Thomas ed. Emmos, Robert A. and Hill, Joanna, *Words of Gratitude* (Philadelphia: Templeton Foundation Press, 2001), p. 14.

Chapter 3

1. Tolstaya, Tatyana, "See the Other Side," *The New Yorker*, March 12, 2007.

Chapter 6

1. http://en.wikipedia.org/wiki/Marian_a_Trench.

Chapter 8

1. http://www.values.com/inspirational-sayings-billboards/51-Charity.

Chapter 9

1. http://forums.doghouseboxing.com/index.php?showtopic=164285.

Chapter 11

1. http://www.moreillustrations.com/Illustrations/tithing%201.html.

Chapter 12

1. http://www.preceptaustin.org/ephesians_318-19.htm.

About the Author

A popular speaker at churches and leading conferences such as Catalyst and Thrive, Margaret Feinberg was recently named one of the "30 Voices" who will help lead the church in the next decade by *Charisma* magazine. She has written more than two dozen books and Bible studies, including the critically acclaimed *The Organic God*, *The Sacred Echo*, *Scouting the Divine*, and their corresponding DVD Bible studies. She is known for her relational teaching style and inviting people to discover the relevance of God and His Word in a modern world.

Margaret and her books have been covered by national media, including: CNN, the Associated Press, *Los Angeles Times*, Dallas Morning News, *Washington Post*, *Chicago Tribune*, and many others. She currently lives in Colorado, with her 6'8" husband, Leif, and superpup, Hershey. Go ahead, become her friend on Facebook, follow her on Twitter @mafeinberg, add her on Google+ or check out her website at www.margaretfeinberg.com.